Belair Early Years

Music

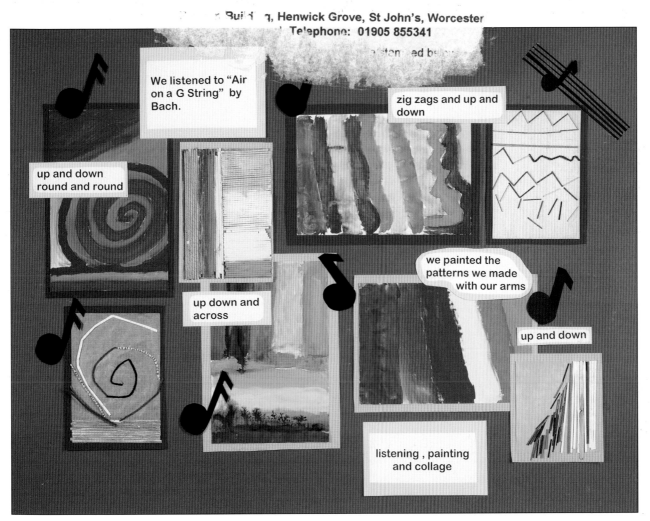

We listened to "Air on a G String" by Bach.

up and down round and round

zig zags and up and down

up down and across

we painted the patterns we made with our arms

up and down

listening, painting and collage

Julie Morrow

Acknowledgements

The author and the publishers would like to thank the following for their invaluable help and support during the preparation of this book:

● the staff and children of Stoneygate Playgroup

● the staff and children of Stoneygate Nursery School

● Jean Hartley, Elaine Edwards and David Ware

● West Orange Recording Studio.

The author would also like to thank Colin and Rosa Robb for the grandfather clock, music box and wooden tabletop with pointer.

For my daughter, Ailsa.

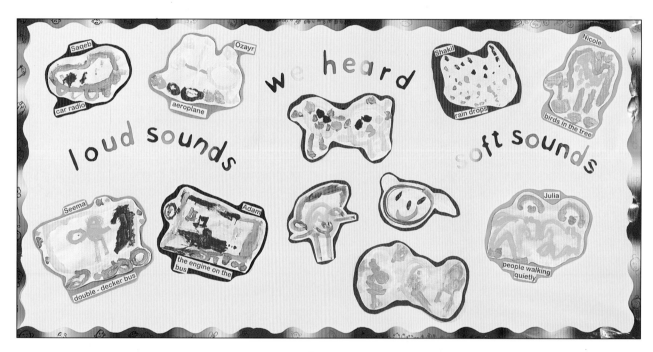

Dynamics (page 33)

First published in 2000 by Belair Publications.
Apex Business Centre, Boscombe Road, Dunstable, LU5 4RL.
Email: belair@belair-publications.co.uk

Editor: Elizabeth Miles   Design: Jane Conway   Cover design: Ed Gallagher
Layout artist: Phillipa Jarvis   Photography: Roger Brown and Kelvin Freeman

© 2000 Belair Publications, on behalf of the author.
Reprinted 2001.
Reprinted 2004.

British Library Cataloguing in Publication Data. A catalogue record for this publication is available from the British Library.

ISBN 0 94788 246-4

Contents

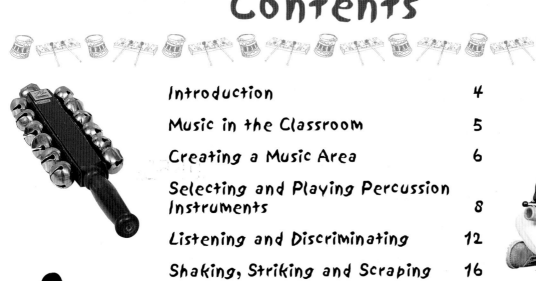

Introduction

I like to play the drum

The aim of this series is to provide resource material covering all the main areas of young children's learning. Each book is a 64-page full colour resource, designed specifically for educators, which provides practical 'hands on' activities suitable for working with the under-fives. They also provide a variety of starting points to encourage and promote creative play.

Written by professionals working in early years education, each book is organised into popular early years themes providing ideas to develop the linguistic, mathematical, scientific, creative, environmental, and personal and social areas of learning. The key learning intentions are provided for each theme.

Full colour photography offers ideas and inspiration for presenting and developing children's individual work with creative ideas for display. An additional feature of each book is the 'Home Links' section. This provides extension ideas and activities for children to develop at home for each theme.

Children enjoy making music and taking part in musical activities. A balanced programme of music education can be devised by including activities from each section of this book. All the activities have been tried and approved by staff working with children aged from three to five years. Adults leading the sessions do not need any special musical ability themselves.

Most of the activities are suitable for individuals and small groups, and so encourage the children's personal and social development. Practical music sessions involving large groups rarely work so well because young children can lose concentration and interest if they have to wait too long to join in.

Learning Intentions

The lists of learning intentions in *Music* will help adults to evaluate the children's progress with reference to specific achievements. By referring to these goals, the children can also be praised in a meaningful way, for example: 'Well done! You told me which chime bar is higher' or 'That was good playing! You played quietly when the conductor told you to'. Children's achievements can be recorded in 'achievement portfolios' by writing a description of their achievement alongside a photograph or by including a piece of their own writing or a drawing.

When music is planned with clear objectives, links to other areas of the curriculum and the importance of music to the development of young children will become apparent.

Music in the Classroom

Music is such an important part of our culture and development it should not be confined to one classroom area or to particular sessions. Here are some examples of other ways to use music in the classroom:

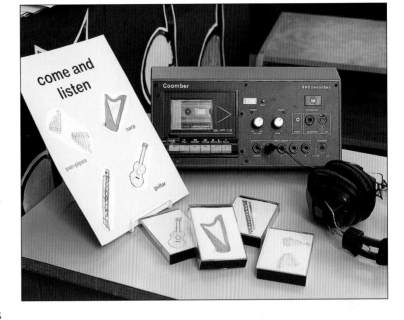

- Use distinct pieces of music as cues for routine activities, such as tidying up and lining up at the door. Make sure the music is not too loud or exciting. Introduce the pieces one at a time and tell the children what they are going to be used for.

- Use calming music at the end of physical sessions such as Movement and Physical Education. If the children lie still and listen for just two minutes they will be calmer when it is time to get dressed.

- Use music in the art area. Put a few different pieces of music featuring different instruments onto individual tapes. Label each cassette box with an illustration of the instrument, such as a classical guitar, piano, cello, flute, church organ, steel drums and sitar. Encourage the children to choose a tape to play while they are painting.

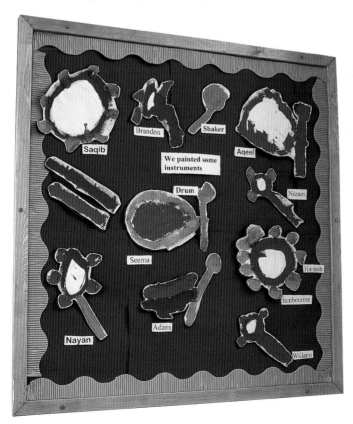

- Place instruments in the painting area and talk about the features of a chosen instrument. Encourage the children to draw an instrument from careful observation.

- Put tapes of music from different cultures in the role-play area. Introduce photographs, pictures and items of clothing associated with the music.

Creating a Music Area

Learning Intentions

- To experiment by selecting, playing and listening to different instruments.

- To concentrate on an activity of their choice.

- To work alongside other children.

- To extend their vocabulary through various activities.

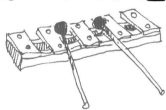

- Design a music area within the classroom or in a space near to the classroom that can be visited regularly. Use two corners of the room and make a square or rectangular area by adding cupboards or shelves. This will screen the area and limit access.

- Cover the shelves with materials that will absorb sound when items are put down (for example, cork tiles or carpet tiles).

- Put carpet on the floor area and carpet squares on the walls. The wall carpets will absorb sound and can be used as display boards.

- Monitor the use of the music area by supplying name cards for each child to put on a noticeboard when they are in the area. Limit the number of spaces on the noticeboard to avoid overcrowding in the area. Provide a post box for them to place their names when they have finished.

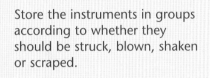

Store the instruments in groups according to whether they should be struck, blown, shaken or scraped.

- Consider which instruments will be available in the area at all times. Begin with a small number of basic instruments (see pages 8–9).

- Encourage the children to sort the instruments according to different criteria. See what criteria the children can think of.

- Introduce the instruments to the children, showing them how to hold each instrument, how to play it and how to take care of it (see pages 8–9).

- Encourage the children to experiment with the instruments. How many different sounds can they make with one instrument?

- Display a clear, visual notice by the entrance, showing the children how many can work in the area at one time.

- Provide a work surface covered with carpet on which the children can place equipment such as chime bars. Add a bookstand for music.

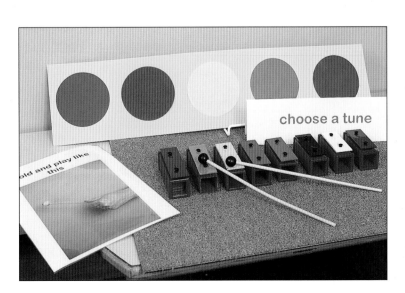

choose a tune

hold and play like this

Home Links

Ask parents or carers to:

- choose a suitable place for their children to play and store some musical instruments

- help their children to explore the different sounds that can be made with an instrument

- encourage their children to put away one instrument before getting out another.

Selecting and Playing Percussion Instruments

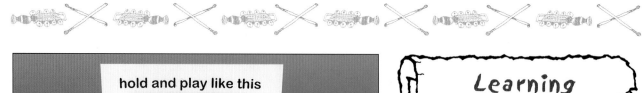

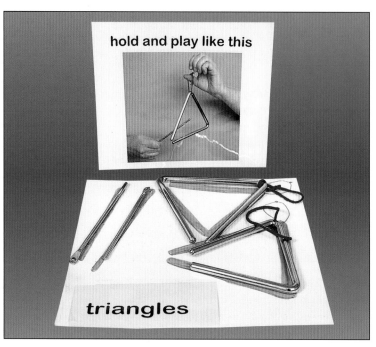

hold and play like this

triangles

Learning Intentions

- To handle instruments carefully.

- To choose instruments from a wide selection.

- To replace instruments after use.

- To hold instruments correctly to ensure that a good quality and broad range of sound is produced.

Triangles

- Provide at least two different sizes of triangle to demonstrate the effect size has on pitch and quality of sound.

- Demonstrate the correct playing technique. Put your thumb, fleshy part up, into the string loop. Hold the triangle beater loosely between the fingers and thumb of the other hand, with the thumbnail facing upwards. Tap the inside of the triangle to prevent too much movement.

- Experiment with the production of sound. What happens if the children hold the triangle instead of the string?

- Experiment with the beater. It should bounce lightly from the triangle when the triangle is tapped. If the children have the beater in their fist, the triangle will not produce a clear, resonant sound.

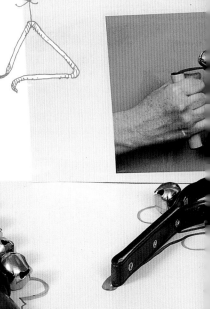

hold and p

bells

When not in use, hang triangles on a hook at the back or side of a shelf. Coat the string loop with plastic tape on the side that fits over the thumb. Stencil the shelf so the correct triangle will be put in place. Allow spaces for beaters.

Chime Bars

- If possible, use colour-coded chime bars. Provide rubber-headed beaters to reduce the noise.

- Teach the children to hold the chimes at the base, or place them on a surface. The beater should be held with the thumbnail up.

- The beater should bounce lightly from the chime bar. Practise this technique to get the best sound effects.

- Practise matching individual colour circles to individual chime bars.

- Examine the design of the chime bars. Remove the bars and play them on a different surface. Experiment and try to make different sounds.

To store chime bars, make a stencil so that the children can replace the bars easily. This also helps them to match colour and size. Add a selection of beaters and provide a diagram showing how they should be held.

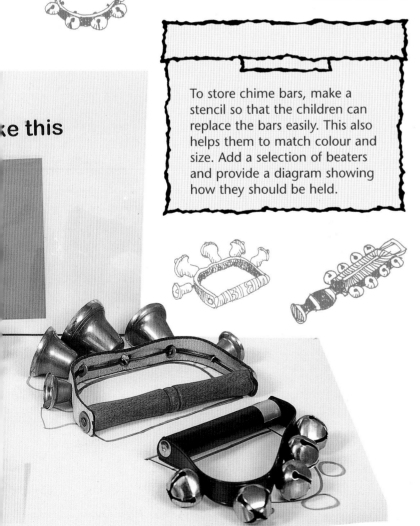

Bells

Display a selection of different types of bells on one shelf, such as jingle sticks and sleigh bells.

- Examine different designs. Sort the bells according to shape, size and materials.

- Hold the bells firmly, gripping them with the whole hand. Practise shaking them quickly and slowly, both while moving and while standing still.

- Discuss where else the children may have heard bells like these (Santa's sleigh, on donkeys or horses, etc.).

- Dance while wearing wrist and ankle bells.

ke this

Tambours and Tambourines

- Provide a tambour and tambourine to give an opportunity to introduce the language concept of 'with and without'. The tambour is the same shape and design as the tambourine but is 'without' the metal discs around the outside.

- Teach the children the correct playing technique by putting the thumb through a hole in the side of the instrument. Close the hand to grip it. Use the other hand to tap or beat the instrument. A beater with a felt head will make a soft sound on the tambour.

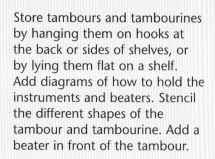

Store tambours and tambourines by hanging them on hooks at the back or sides of shelves, or by lying them flat on a shelf. Add diagrams of how to hold the instruments and beaters. Stencil the different shapes of the tambour and tambourine. Add a beater in front of the tambour.

Shakers and Maracas

- Provide a selection of home-made and professionally made instruments.

- Teach the children to play one maraca in each hand, alternating the beats.

Store shakers and maracas together on one shelf, using stencils.

Wood Blocks

- Provide a selection of wood blocks of different sizes and shapes and keep them together on the same shelf.

- Once children have learned how to hold the beater correctly, it is difficult to play these incorrectly. The beater should bounce lightly from the block when struck.

- Sort the blocks according to criteria decided during discussion with the children. Talk about the shape and design of the blocks.

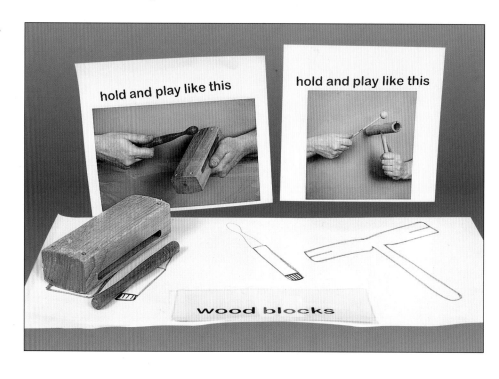

hold and play like this

hold and play like this

wood blocks

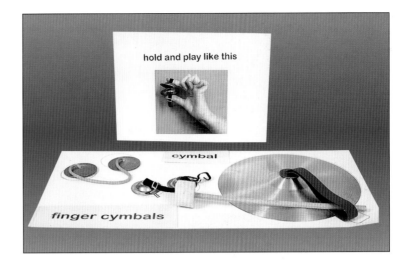

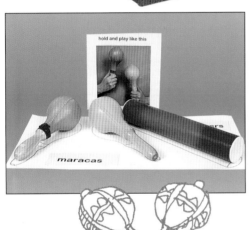

Cymbals and Castanets

● Provide different types of cymbal – a large one with a single beater, and small pairs.

● Experiment with the technique needed to play one cymbal with a beater. The cymbal must not touch anything when you strike it – what happens if it does?

● Experiment with pairs of cymbals. Encourage the children to practise so that the cymbals bounce away from each other after striking. Listen to the sounds made by releasing or holding the cymbals together after striking.

● Provide a selection of small instruments that are played with the finger and thumb rather than a whole-hand grip, such as finger cymbals and castanets.

● Play the finger cymbals and castanets in the same way as the pairs of cymbals. The sound effects are better if the instruments are released as soon as the two surfaces have touched. Encourage the children to practise this technique.

Cymbals and castanets can be stored on hooks or flat on a shelf over stencils, with diagrams showing how they are held and played.

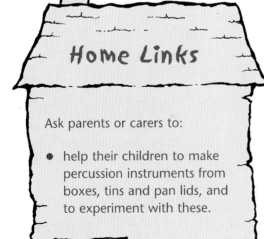

Home Links

Ask parents or carers to:

● help their children to make percussion instruments from boxes, tins and pan lids, and to experiment with these.

Other Instruments

● As well as the basic instruments that are always available, it is a good idea to keep a space for a variety of new instruments for the children to try.

Listening and Discriminating

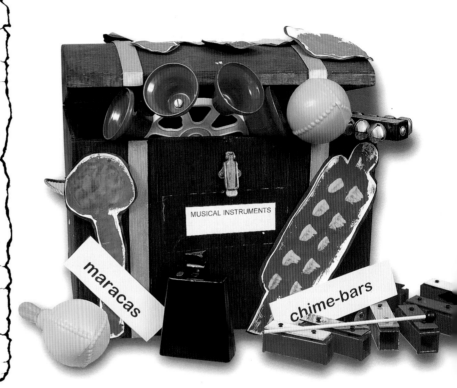

Learning Intentions

- To concentrate on the differences between particular sounds and to develop listening skills in a quiet environment.

- To understand that different instruments make different sounds.

- To recognise the sound and description of different instruments.

- To know the names of percussion instruments.

Starting Points

Use a portable music box for sessions that take place outside the music area. The music box could contain: a pair of cymbals, a triangle and beater, a tambourine, a tambour, a pair of maracas, a jingle stick, sleigh bells, a wood block and beater, two-tone wood block and beater, castanets and finger cymbals.

- Hold regular listening sessions so that the children get used to listening quietly.

- Put a picture of every instrument on the lid of the music box so that you can check all have been replaced at the end of a session.

- Start with short sessions in which you take out the instruments and play them. Emphasise their names and how to hold them.

- Use the instruments to accompany pieces of music, up to two minutes in length, with a strong beat.

- Encourage the children to handle the instruments carefully.

- Give each child an instrument. Name an instrument and the child who has it puts it away in the box. You can also use pictures to help those children who cannot remember the names.

- To develop vocabulary skills, describe the instrument by the way it is played. For example: 'If you shake/strike/scrape your instrument, put it in the box now.'

Guessing Games

- Place a variety of percussion instruments in a large lidded box. Encourage the children to sing or chant the following rhyme:

  'Here is a box, a music box,
  Full up with things to play.
  Here is a box, a music box
  Let's see what is in it today!'

  Lift the lid of the box and play an instrument behind the lid so that the children cannot see it. Ask them to guess the instrument. When a child guesses correctly, give him or her the instrument to play.

  If the children cannot name the instruments, supply a choice of picture cards for them to point to instead.

- Make a screen to hide the instruments from view by opening out a large cardboard box or by hinging together two pieces of wood. Decorate the screen with pictures of instruments painted by the children.

  Place a selection of instruments behind the screen and encourage the children to take turns to go behind the screen. Ask the child behind the screen to play an instrument of their choice. The other children take turns to guess which instrument is being played by pointing to the picture card or by naming the instrument. Another child takes a turn behind the screen when he or she identifies an instrument correctly.

- Extend these activities by playing instruments that make similar sounds, such as bells and tambourines.

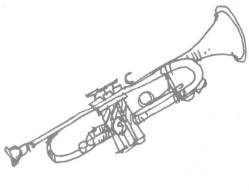

Puppet Role-play

- Use a glove puppet to play the instruments behind and above the screen during a guessing game (see page 13).

  Introduce the puppet to the children and tell them her name. Ask her if she has some things to play with behind the screen. She will 'tell' you and the children that she has some instruments.

- You can use a conversation with the puppet to show the children that she often does not listen carefully, and gets distracted by waving at them. Eventually she will show the children the instruments she has got, but only if they can guess what they are first.

- Ask the puppet if she has a particular instrument, such as a tambour. She will tell you that she thinks so, and will play it behind the screen. The children have to decide if she is playing the right one.

- Let each child have a turn at asking the puppet if she has a specific instrument. Remind them to praise the puppet if she shows them the correct one. She will then pass the instruments over the screen after playing them.

- Finish the puppet session by letting the puppet 'conduct' the children as they play and sing a song of their choice.

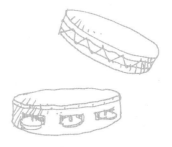

Listening Games

- Make up to 18 short recordings (each of 2–3 seconds) of percussion instruments in random order.

  Divide a circular board or card into six sections. Put an arrow in the middle and an instrument that corresponds with those on the tape into each section of the circle.

  Play the tape but pause after each short recording. The children must point the arrow to the instrument they think they have heard. Continue until they have matched all the short recordings with the correct instruments.

- Give a group of six children a percussion instrument each. Play longer (10-second) recordings of each instrument. When a child recognises their own instrument they must join in by playing it. If they do not recognise their instrument, prompt them by pointing the arrow to their instrument.

- Fill some containers with items that sound very different when shaken, such as dried beans, dry sand, discarded pieces of wax crayon, milk bottle tops, paper straw pieces and nails. Put the same item in two of the containers. Seal the containers and ask the children to find the two that are the same.

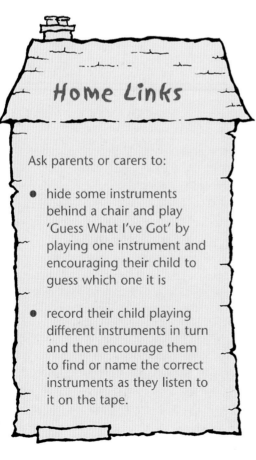

Home Links

Ask parents or carers to:

- hide some instruments behind a chair and play 'Guess What I've Got' by playing one instrument and encouraging their child to guess which one it is

- record their child playing different instruments in turn and then encourage them to find or name the correct instruments as they listen to it on the tape.

Shaking, Striking and Scraping

Learning Intentions

- To know that different materials can make different sounds.

- To understand that the sound of instruments can be changed by varying the quantity and type of materials used to make them.

- To understand the meaning of terms such as 'same as' and 'different'.

- To create their own instruments and to experiment with various materials.

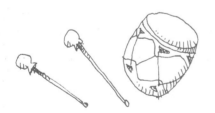

Starting Points

- Set up an instrument workshop area. Begin by providing materials to make instruments (see below).

- Within the workshop, set up a working area from which the children can see and reach all the materials.

- Introduce the children to the area and develop the activities over several weeks, so that there is plenty of time to experiment with different fillings and containers. Provide ready-made instruments as stimuli.

- Discuss how instruments can be played in different ways. Demonstrate shaking, striking and scraping various instruments. Which works best and why?

Instruments to Strike

- Make instruments to strike, using containers such as boxes or tins. Use the container's lid for striking or make a drum skin by putting baking parchment or Cellophane over the top and attaching with an elastic band. Decorate as desired.

- Make beaters by drilling holes into rubber balls or by cutting into foam balls with scissors. Fix dowelling into the holes with PVA glue.

- Decorate the instruments as desired.

Instruments to Shake

- Encourage the children to fill similar containers, such as lidded plastic tubs, with different materials. Shake them and compare the sounds. Try dried beans, dry sand, discarded pieces of wax crayons, milk bottle tops, paper straw pieces and nails.

- Tape a small amount of the filling, or a picture of the filling, to the base of each container. Ask the children to find two that sound the same. Turn these upside down to see if they are correct.

- Encourage the children to choose from different containers (plastic bottles, cylindrical containers, small plastic pots, cardboard boxes), to fill one with their chosen material and seal it. Attach a stick with tape to the instrument for a handle.

- Decorate instruments made from plastic containers with paints mixed with PVA glue. Instruments made from transparent bottles are attractive if a variety of coloured fillings are used.

Instruments to Scrape

- Make instruments to scrape with wood, corrugated card, sandpaper or plastic bottles with ridged surfaces. Glue pieces of corrugated card or sandpaper onto blocks of wood or onto the outside of containers.

- Use a variety of sticks (wood, plastic and metal) to scrape the instruments.

- Decorate the instruments as desired.

Home Links

Ask parents or carers to:

- collect containers for their children to bring into the instrument workshop

- discuss with their children what sort of instrument they could make with a particular container

- help their children compare the sounds of home-made or manufactured instruments.

Listening and Responding

Learning Intentions

- To develop listening skills.

- To memorise the words and actions of a rhyme and to develop an awareness of sequence.

- To identify sounds and to know that different objects can make different sounds.

- To use memory and listening skills to recall and identify familiar sounds.

- To represent sounds heard in the environment, with objects and instruments.

Starting Points

- Ask a musician (perhaps a parent) to play the first lines of a song the children know well. Tell the children to listen carefully and to guess what the song is. When they guess correctly, they can sing the song with the musician.

- Use a timing device to guess a song within a specific time period.

Responding

- Learn this action rhyme which can be sung to the tune of 'Baa Baa Black Sheep':

  Stretch up high as tall as a house, *(reach up)*
  Curl up small like a little mouse. *(curl up)*
  Now pretend you have a drum, *(hold imaginary sticks)*
  Play like this: boom boom boom! *(alternate imaginary sticks with each boom)*
  Shake your fingers, *(shake fingers)*
  Stamp your feet, *(stamp)*
  Close your eyes tightly, *(head on hands and eyes closed)*
  And go to sleep. *(keep eyes closed and be quiet)*

- Paint pictures to illustrate the rhyme. Display it so that the children can check the sequence of lines as they perform the rhyme.

Capture the Treasure

- Fill a 'treasure chest' with a variety of 'noisy treasures', such as scrunched-up gold-coloured Cellophane (gold), a packet of crispy snacks (sailors' rations), a bunch of keys (keys to the treasure chest), coins in a net bag. Then encourage the children to handle the objects and listen to the noises they make.

- Play 'Capture the Treasure'. One child goes on guard, sitting with their back to the treasure chest, while the others take turns to tiptoe to the chest and try to remove some treasure. If the guard hears and names the object being handled, the others must put back the treasure. The aim is to capture all the treasure without the guard hearing.

Our World Sounds

- Visit a park or railway station to identify and record sounds. Follow some sounds to their source and tape-record them (for example, park sounds: birds singing, ducks quacking, a fountain, footsteps on dry leaves; railway sounds: trains, doors shutting, whistles).

- Ask the children to listen to the recorded sounds. Ask: 'How were the sounds made?' 'Can you make the sounds yourselves with your voices or with instruments?'

- Make a chart showing the sequence of the visit and the sounds heard. Tell and re-tell the story of your visit, using the chart to prompt, and ask the children to make the sounds themselves.

- Paint pictures of the sources of the sounds and label them to make a display. Actual items collected on the visit could be added, together with the instruments used to reproduce the sounds.

In the park

birds sing

ducks splash

Leaves crunch

your fingers   Stamp your feet   close your eyes tightly   and go to sleep

Home Links

Ask parents or carers to:

- play 'What am I Going to Sing?' by humming the first few notes of a nursery rhyme, and asking the children to guess which it is (if necessary, continue with more notes or some words)

- make a tape of sounds from familiar events (for example, the collection of bins, the bath running, pouring cereal into a dish); can the other children guess what the sounds are?

Developing Singing Skills

Learning Intentions

- To enjoy singing by themselves, in groups and from memory.

- To perform actions at the correct point in a song.

- To enjoy producing singing sounds and to copy the pitch and tune of a short phrase.

- To maintain a good posture while singing and to sing with changes of vocal and facial expression.

- To understand that the same song can sound different when sung by different people.

- To develop language and literacy skills through songs.

- To use simple technology in recording and playing songs.

- Begin each new song by singing short sections to the children and asking them to join in. Continue with more sections until the whole song is familiar. Praise any attempts to sing or join in actions.

- Show the children pictures that illustrate the songs. Encourage them to draw their own pictures to represent a song. Build up a display of pictures to help the children choose a song to sing.

Starting Points

- Create a quiet area for singing, with nursery rhyme books, paper, felt-tipped pens or crayons.

- Plan to teach a variety of songs. The list should contain nursery rhymes, action songs ('Here is a Beehive' and 'Heads, Shoulders, Knees and Toes') and counting songs ('Five Little Speckled Frogs' and 'Five Little Ducks'). Aim to teach at least one new song each week.

- Link songs to project work on animals or farms, for example: 'Old Macdonald' and 'Dingle Dangle Scarecrow'.

- Teach the songs in small groups, for around ten minutes at a time. Singing together in larger groups is fun, but only when children can already sing the song and feel safe.

twinkle, twinkle

build a little house

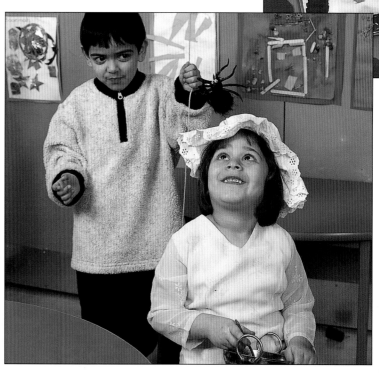

Recording

- Show the children how to operate a simple tape recorder by recording some singing, rewinding and playing it back.

- Ask the children to select a song from the display and sing a little of it. Record each attempt. Play these back and ask the children to show you or tell you the name of the song.

- Record the tune to a song the children are learning. Small groups of children can listen and sing along to the tape. Less confident children may find it easier to make a glove puppet 'sing' for them.

Language and Literacy

- Gather together some percussion instruments that have three-syllable names (tambourine, triangle, big bass drum, jingle bells). Sit a small group of children in a circle and let each child choose an instrument. Sing 'Who has got a tambourine?' to the tune of 'Twinkle, Twinkle, Little Star'. The child with the tambourine will sing and play 'I have got a tambourine', and so on.

- Repeat the above activity but use objects or pictures linked to a current topic, such as three-syllable animals (for example, crocodile, elephant).

- Act out 'Five Little Frogs' as it is sung, encouraging five children to 'jump into the pool' in turn.

- Act out 'Little Miss Muffett' as it is sung. Put a toy spider on a long piece of string and thread the string through a hook on the wall. One child sits under the spider as 'Miss Muffett' while another lowers and raises the spider.

21

Different Voices

- Visit various locations indoors and outdoors, such as a church, hall, subway, tunnel or under a bridge. Let the children take turns, singing and listening to the sound. Ask the listeners to tell you about the sounds they can hear. Can they hear an echo?

- Record a selection of voices singing the same song, including male and female adult and child singers (a local operatic group or choir may help). Take photographs of the singers and see if the children can match the picture to the voice.

- Discuss the similarities and differences between the voices, introducing vocabulary such as 'deep, 'low' and 'high'.

- Extend this into a simple lotto game using a board showing the singers' photographs.

Distance and Clarity

- After singing sitting down, ask the children to stand up and sing. Discuss the difference in how their voices sound. Encourage good posture by modelling a straight back, shoulders down and relaxed, and hands held loosely by the sides. Guard against raised shoulders by asking the children to pretend they have a heavy bucket in each hand.

- Sing with wide-open mouths and contrast this with singing through almost closed mouths.

- Give a group of children a 'message' to sing. Ask them to stand some distance away and sing the message sitting down while looking at the floor, and then standing up while looking at the listeners. Which was easier to hear?

- Ask the children to draw pictures of children singing with open mouths.

Composition

- Make up a song together, based on a shared experience. It can be sung using two or more notes. Use a well-known tune, such as the first line of 'Bye Baby Bunting'. Let the children take turns in making up the next line of the song. For example:

  'We went to the pet shop
  It was very busy.
  We looked for some
  goldfish food,
  But there wasn't any!'

- Write down and illustrate any popular songs that you make up for display.

- Make up a string of words beginning with the same letter. Sing these to a familiar tune. Display the words with a selection of objects beginning with the same letter.

- Make up a string of words that have the same number of beats (sounds). Sing these to a familiar tune. Display the song with objects or pictures of items that have the same number of beats in their names.

Expression

- Tell a story that includes phrases that the children like to join in with (such as 'Three Little Pigs'). When you tell the story, sing the catch phrases and encourage the children to do the same.

- After you have sung the phrase, ask the children to think of words to describe your expression. Sing the same phrase but with a different expression. Talk about the changes they can see, then ask them to paint or draw them.

- Ask the children to categorise songs that they know by the feelings that the songs create or explore. Make lists of these songs and ask the children to illustrate them for display.

Home Links

Ask parents or carers to:

- visit their local library and borrow some recordings of different singing styles to play and discuss with their children

- sing to their children when carrying out daily routines such as washing and dressing, trying to match the song to the activity.

Developing Awareness of Rhythm and Beat

Learning Intentions

- To know that some pieces of music have regular beats that can be counted.

- To understand a variety of directions.

- To know how to alternate their hands while playing a regular beat.

- To recognise, name and respond to different beats.

- To discriminate between beats that are different in pace and volume.

- To accompany different beats accurately.

Music and Rhymes

- Make a model of a grandfather clock with a movable pendulum. Teach the children 'Hickory Dickory Dock', using the model so the children can see the pendulum go back and forth in time to the music. Ask them to copy the action with one arm.

- Introduce a 'stop' command, saying it and using a simple hand signal for reinforcement. Encourage the children to swing their arms and stop on command.

- When children can beat in time with the pendulum, introduce two-tone wood blocks. More able children will be able to use these to alternate the beats.

- Listen for the 'tick-tock' beat in other short pieces of music.

soft
slow
smooth

Starting Points

- Introduce the idea of a beat by playing some music and tapping or clapping to the beat. Demonstrate the regular pattern of the beat, with some beats emphasised. Ask the children to join in with percussion instruments.

- Talk about activities that seem to have a beat, such as running, walking, skipping and dancing.

- Listen to a short piece of music that has a slow, regular walking beat. Invite the children to join in with the beat by 'walking' their hands. They can then stand up and walk around the room, moving their feet to the beat. Extend by playing music that has a faster beat.

- Make a tape with short pieces of music with frequently changing beats. Can the children recognise and react to running and walking beats? Introduce a skipping beat using the same approach.

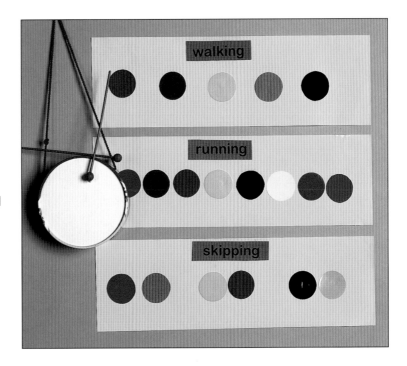

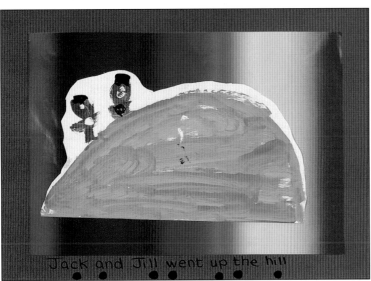

- Using pictures and tapes of familiar nursery rhymes, work out which have walking/marching or skipping beats. (Rhymes with walking/marching beats: 'Grand Old Duke of York', 'Baa Baa Black Sheep', 'Polly Put the Kettle On', 'Mary Mary'; rhymes with skipping beats: 'Here We Go Round the Mulberry Bush, Humpty Dumpty, Jack and Jill, Pat-a-cake.)

- Introduce symbols for beats, such as coloured circles, bottle tops, buttons or circles of fabric. Encourage the children to glue these to strips of card to represent walking, running and skipping beats.

- Ask the children to paint pictures of nursery rhymes and add the relevant beat using symbols. Create a display of rhymes with walking, running and skipping beats.

- Put a tape recorder and instruments in the music area and prompt the children to try to play the different beats on display.

- Demonstrate an object with a 'tick-tock' beat, such as a clockwork egg-timer, clock, watch, wind-up toy or metronome. Encourage the children to think of other items. Collect and display the items.

- Listen to the tick-tock beats. Encourage the children to tap their fingers quietly against their palms as they listen. Do they notice differences in the speed of the beats? Introduce some musical vocabulary ('fast', 'slow', 'loud' and 'soft').

Sequences

- Learn and practise actions in sequences of two (clap, pat), three (clap, pat, stamp) and four (click, clap, pat, stamp). Create silhouettes of hands and feet showing the patterns for the children to follow.

- Use the sequences to accompany songs (two-beat songs: 'This Old Man', 'Polly Put the Kettle On'; three-beat songs: 'Dance to Your Daddy', 'Oranges and Lemons'; four-beat songs: 'Twinkle, Twinkle, Little Star', 'Mary Had a Little Lamb').

- Place two, three or four appropriate instruments in a line and ask the children to repeat the sequence by playing the instruments from left to right (with one child playing each sound). Play two beats (bang, tap); three beats (scrape, bang, tap); or four beats (scrape, bang, tap, jingle).

- Listen to a song or piece of music. Can the children work out which sequence of actions fits the beat? Try 'Hot Cross Buns' (four beats), 'London's Burning' (three beats) and 'Row Your Boat' (two beats).

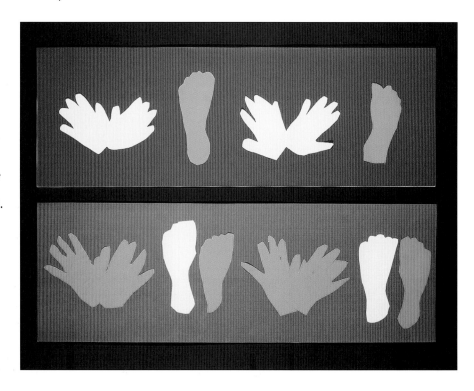

- On a tape recorder, play a piece of music with a strong beat, such as a march. Divide the children into players and marchers. Players strike percussion instruments with a hand or with beaters for the marchers to march in time. Play the tape and let the children take turns to march and play.

- When you are sure that most of the children can keep to the beat, tell them that they should try to continue the beat unaided, and turn down the volume on your player for a few seconds. Gradually increase the length of time you keep the sound down. How long can they keep going?

- Let the players watch the feet of the marchers. While the players tap their fingers quietly to the music, let the marchers march out of the room. Turn the music down so that the players can just keep time. Watch the marchers through the window and see how long they can keep to the beat.

Home Links

Ask parents or guardians to:

- play some of their children's favourite songs and to encourage them to move in time to the beats (walking, running or skipping)

- do some familiar everyday activities (such as dusting, sweeping or hammering) in time to music

- help their children to make a list of the different beats heard around the house – are the beats fast or slow?

Rhythmic Patterns

Learning Intentions

- To recognise the rhythmic pattern of long and short sounds in music and speech.

- To know that words are made up of different sounds and have different numbers of beats. To understand that words have distinct patterns.

- To understand that the sounds/syllables in words can be represented by beats.

- To beat or clap up to five-sound patterns.

- To count sounds and sort words according to the number of beats.

- To recall a name and think and play its pattern without saying it.

Starting Points

- Collect and introduce four glove- or finger-puppets to represent names with one, two, three and four sounds (for example Pat, Sophie, Shaheeda and Annabella). Every time the puppet is shown to the children, encourage them to greet it by saying and clapping its name.

- Try the above activity using the children's own names. First let the whole group clap the same name, then go round in a circle, letting each child clap his or her own name.

- Illustrate the children's name cards with dots to show the number of sounds in their name.

- Make animal-shaped name cards to illustrate the number of sounds in names. For example, use elephant-shaped cards for three-sound names and hippo-shaped cards for four-sound names.

- When the children can imitate different rhythmic patterns accurately, help them to count the beats. Then ask them to think of a two-, three- or four-beat name and clap it.

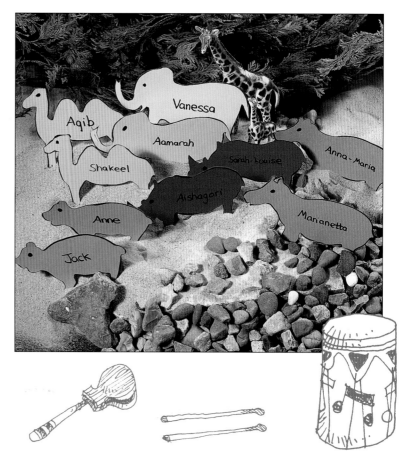

- Extend the previous activity by thinking of words that relate to a chosen topic. Draw pictures to illustrate them. Help the children to sort the pictures into piles of one-, two-, three- and four-syllable words. Write the words on the pictures for the children, and help them to stick spots underneath, one for each syllable in the word.

- Make a block graph to display words of one, two, three and four syllables.

Counting the Beats ♩. ♪ ♫ ♩

- When the children can imitate rhythmic patterns of two-, three-, four- and five-beat words, encourage them to count the beats as they clap.

- Ask the children to clap two, three, four or five beats. Then ask them to tell you how many beats there are in a selection of different words. Encourage them to clap each word to find out.

- Ask children to sort model vehicles or animals into sets according to the number of beats in their names. Draw one, two and three circles on cards so that the models with one beat can be put on the card with one circle, the models with two can be put on the card with two circles, and so on.

- Make a block graph by lining objects above a number and symbol according to how many beats they have (see photograph above).

Matching Games

- Make a selection of picture cards representing words that have one, two, three and four syllables, for example, 'vehicle' picture cards could include car, van; scooter, tractor; motorbike, racing car; and helicopter, car transporter. Discuss the number of beats in the words with the children and add the corresponding number of spots to the back of each card.

- Children can sort the cards into piles, according to the number of beats and then check whether they were correct by looking at the back of each card.

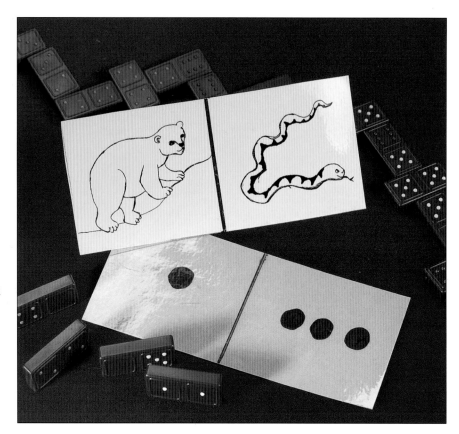

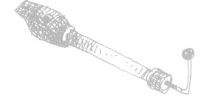

- Play 'Snap'. Children say 'Snap!' and win the cards if they correctly match the number of beats on their card to the number of beats on the card they can see.

- Put two pictures on longer strips of card with the corresponding number of dots on the reverse to create dominoes. Play dominoes by matching pictures that have the same number of beats. Encourage the children to look at the number of dots on the back to check they have been matched correctly.

- Play 'lotto' by giving the children boards with four spaces, each with a number of dots. Give each child some picture cards representing different numbers of beats. Play a number of beats on a drum. The children must match the number of beats to the correct picture and place the picture on their board.

Spin and Play

- Make a circle with card or wood and attach an arrow-shaped spinner at the centre. Divide the circle into six sections and place an object or picture in each. Take turns to spin the arrow. When it stops the children must try to say and clap the pattern of the word.

- Vary the above activity by letting the children play the beats with beaters on wood blocks.

Home Links

Ask parents or carers to:

- encourage their children to clap the patterns of the names of some of their favourite toys

- ask their children to give them a toy with a two-, three- or four-beat name from a selection of three, without saying the name – instead just clapping the number of beats.

Song Patterns

- Learn the pattern of a part of a song or rhyme. For example:

  'Wheels On the Bus', 'Head and Shoulders, Knees and Toes' and 'Jingle Bells'.

- Encourage the children to repeat the pattern (clapping or tapping) and to keep this going while listening to a tape of the song.

- Divide the group into singers and players – one group sings the song, the other plays the rhythm pattern.

- Try singing and playing together. Use instruments suitable for the song, such as bells for 'Jingle Bells' and a scraper for 'Wheels On the Bus'.

Dynamics

Learning Intentions

- To know that sounds can be loud or soft.

- To understand the concepts of loud and soft.

- To adapt their own playing to the volume of a piece of music.

- To identify loud and soft sounds.

Starting Points

- Introduce a 'listening time'. Play short pieces of loud and soft music and some pieces of music with frequent changes of dynamics. Discuss each piece and encourage the children to use appropriate vocabulary, such as 'loud', 'soft', 'getting softer', 'getting louder'.

- Listen to a short piece of loud music. Tap toes to the beat and then play a percussion instrument with the music. Repeat with a short piece of quiet music.

- Play a new piece of music and ask the children to decide how to play along. After they have played, ask them if the music was loud or soft.

- Encourage the children to move according to the dynamics of a piece of music, for example stamping and tiptoeing as necessary.

Sounds Around

- Take the children on a walk indoors or outdoors, where you are likely to hear different sounds. Stop and listen. Ask the children if they can hear any loud sounds. Trace these to their source and ask the children to draw what they can see. Repeat for soft sounds.

- Make a display of the children's 'loud' and 'soft' sound pictures. Point to a picture and ask the children to make the sounds (see photograph on page 33).

- Play a walking beat on the floor with your hands. Tell the children that this is the sound of an elephant walking and that the elephant is getting nearer (increase the volume, eventually beating loudly). Then gradually let the elephant walk away, until it is so far away that you cannot hear it any more and there is silence.

- Build this activity into short stories about animals moving about in a forest.

- Make a display of pictures of animals which might walk loudly and animals which might walk softly.

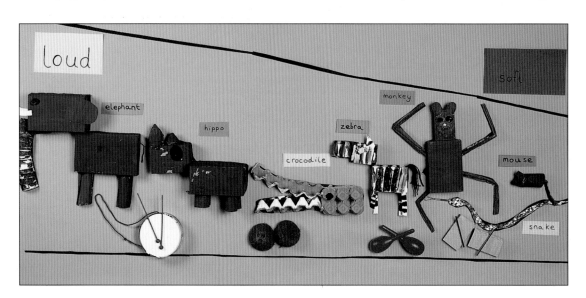

The display board reads: loud sounds / we heard / soft sounds

Labels: Saqeb — car radio; Ozayr — aeroplane; Shakil — rain drops; Nicole — birds in the tree; Seema; Adam — the engine on the bus; double-decker bus; Julia — people walking quietly

Three Billy Goats

● Tell the story of the *Three Billy Goats Gruff* and let the children act it out, using PE equipment for the bridge. Emphasise the difference in the sound made by each Billy Goat on the bridge (very soft, very loud and in-between).

● Make four cards, one for the troll and one for each Billy Goat. Four children select a card each. The one who picks the troll card hides under the 'bridge'. In turn, the others show their card to the children who are watching, but not the troll. They will cross the bridge making the sound shown on their card according to the size of the Billy Goat. If the troll guesses the Billy Goat correctly because the sound they make is accurate, they can cross the bridge.

Home Links

Ask parents or carers to:

● stand outdoors with their children, naming any sounds and deciding whether they are loud or soft

● find the source of some of the sounds (if indoor sounds seemed soft from outside; are they still soft when you are near them inside?).

Tempo

Learning Intentions

- To understand and respond to the terms: 'fast', 'faster', 'slow', 'slower' and 'stop'.

- To use the words 'running' and 'walking' to describe fast and slow beats.

Starting Points

- Ask the children to select a percussion instrument. Listen to a short piece of music and decide if it is a slow (walking) beat or a fast (running) beat. Encourage the children to beat to the music by 'walking' or 'running' their hands.

- Explain that they are going to move their hands first, then stop when the music stops, and think. Prompt this by saying 'now think' when the music has stopped. Ask: 'Was that music fast or slow?' 'Did your hands walk or did they run?'

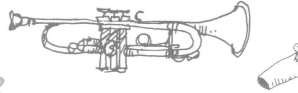

Faster or Slower?

- Play a piece of music that increases or decreases in pace. Encourage the children to move around, matching their own pace with its pace.

- Play the same piece of music. Ask the children to play their percussion instruments along with the music. Stop the tape after there has been a significant increase or decrease in pace. Prompt discussion by saying: 'Tell me what happened when you were playing. Yes, it was fast just now. Was it fast at the beginning? So the music was slow at the beginning and fast at the end – it got faster.'

- Play a walking beat with your hands on the floor. Tell the children that they are going for a walk. Ask them to decide where they are walking to. Slow down or speed up the movement according to where they are going. For example: speed up to cross a road; slow down while you watch a digger on the other side of the road; speed up to catch a bus.

- Make up other commentaries to help the children make a steady beat become faster or slower.

We drew some speed pictures

fast music

slow music

fast and slow music

Getting Faster

- Sing songs with rhythmic actions, such as 'Head, Shoulders, Knees and Toes' and 'Here We Go Round the Mulberry Bush.' Sing the song at the normal pace, then a little faster. Get faster every time you sing it. Can the children keep up with the words and actions together?

- Play traditional dance music that gets faster as the melody is repeated (Greek and Russian dance music for example). Encourage the children to move to the music.

- Draw patterns, such as circles and squiggles, starting slowly and getting faster and faster. Play music while the children draw the appropriate 'speed pictures'.

 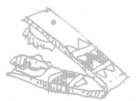

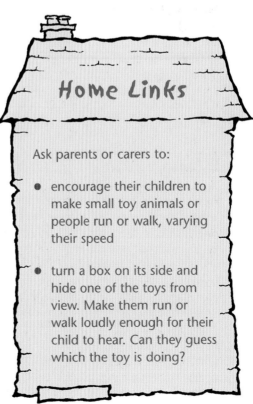

Home Links

Ask parents or carers to:

- encourage their children to make small toy animals or people run or walk, varying their speed

- turn a box on its side and hide one of the toys from view. Make them run or walk loudly enough for their child to hear. Can they guess which the toy is doing?

Duration

Starting Points

- Pass around a triangle. Let each child strike it and then stop the sound by holding the bar. Encourage them to 'stop' the sound on command. Explain that this is a short sound.

- Encourage the children to strike the triangle but not stop the sound and to listen carefully until the sound has gone. Tell the children that these are long sounds.

- Give each child a chime bar. Take turns to play, but do not play until the previous sound has stopped.

Sound Display

- Gather a variety of safe objects that will make a sound when struck. Suspend them with string from hooks attached to a piece of wood balanced over two supports, or tie them to a frame made from construction kit pieces.

- Encourage the children to discover which materials continue to sound after being struck. They can then sort the items into those that make short sounds and those that make long sounds.

- Collect safe pieces of metal (not sharp or rusty). Provide string, staples, pieces of wood and a good selection of materials for children to make their own wind chimes.

Long and Short

- Give each child a kazoo, whistle or similar instrument. Play them together, making long and short sounds.

- Show the children visual signs for long and short. Encourage them to play their instruments, following a sequence of long and short signs.

- Roll a die with long or short words and symbols on it. Children will take turns at playing the sound, following the word or symbol that has landed upright.

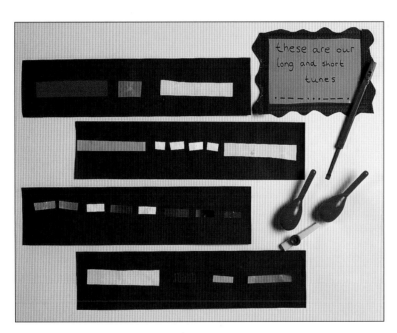

- Draw long and short lines with a thick felt-tipped pen along a piece of card. Label the sounds.

- Sort long and short pieces of paper, card, straws or pipe-cleaners into 'long' and 'short' trays. Choose a selection and glue them in a line onto a piece of card.

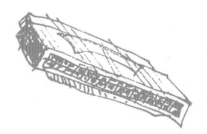

- 'Read' the card from left to right, making the words 'short' and 'long' sound short and long. Encourage the children to play the cards they have made using a variety of instruments that can make long or short sounds, such as sand blocks, whistles, kazoos, triangles, chime bars and scrapers.

- Make a display of the tunes for the children to play.

- Sort instruments that can play long or short sounds, such as recorders, whistles and keyboards, and add them to the display.

Home Links

Ask parents or carers to:

- let their children strike kitchen items, such as bowls, pans and jugs, to discover which make long sounds and which make short sounds.

Pitch

Learning Intentions

- To know the terms 'high', 'higher', 'low', 'lower', 'the same'.

- To understand that adding/ removing liquid alters the pitch of the notes glass jars produce when struck.

- To discriminate between high and low sounds.

- To match the pitch of some notes.

Starting Points

- Place identical thick glass jars and coloured liquid in jugs in the water tray. Also provide metal beaters or teaspoons, plastic jugs and funnels. Help the children to explore what happens to the note when a jar is struck if liquid is added to or taken from a jar. Can they sing the notes?

- Introduce the words 'same' and 'different' while discussing 'quantity' and 'pitch'.

- See if the children can make two identical jars produce the same note. What do they notice about the level of liquid in each?

- Add more jars and fill them with different amounts of water. Line them up and play from left to right to make a simple tune.

We played this tune

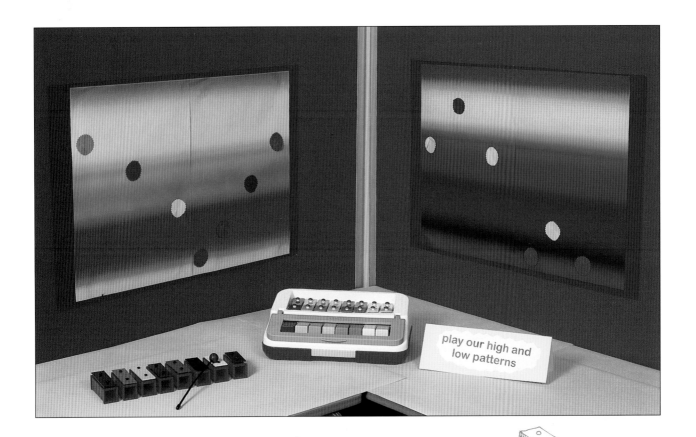

play our high and low patterns

Musical Shapes

- Play a short, slow passage of music that changes pitch. The change should be gradual, like a scale. Talk about what the children heard. Establish whether the piece was high or low at the beginning and what happened next.

- Show the children how this looks on a piece of music, with the pattern of the notes going up or down. Can they draw the pattern of the music in the air with their hands as they listen to it? Then draw the pattern on paper as you listen to the music.

- Ask the children to draw the shapes themselves or to position circles high or low on a piece of paper, according to the pattern. Put the drawings in the music area with a keyboard so that the children can read and play them.

High and Low

- Collect and make a display of items that produce high sounds and items that produce low sounds.

- Ask musicians from a local school or college to bring contrasting high and low instruments (violin/cello, flute/oboe) and let the children hear the differences when the same tune is played.

- Ask the children to move around, making their movements high or low depending on the sound cue from the piano.

Home Links

Ask parents or carers to:

- encourage their children to strike a selection of pots and pans to see if any make the same note

- help their children fill small glass bottles with different amounts of water and experiment to see how the notes change

- fill a large plastic bottle with different quantities of water and let their children blow across the top as though playing a flute.

Conducting and Playing Together

Learning Intentions

- To know the meaning of 'leader'/'conductor', 'band', 'orchestra' and 'musicians'.

- To understand the meaning of various directions, including 'hands quiet'.

- To respond to verbal and visual directions.

- To begin to play co-operatively in a group.

Starting Points

- Ask the children to wait quietly by using the 'hands quiet' direction. Follow with a request to 'listen' and then play some music.

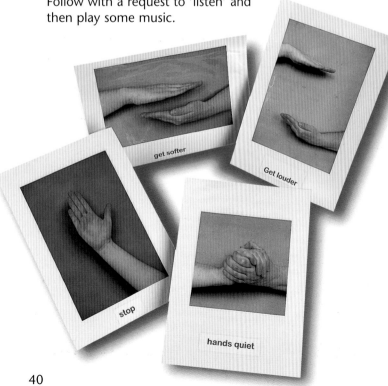

- Teach the children to use and follow some additional standard hand signals. For example: 'stop', 'hands quiet', 'get louder' and 'get softer'. Display the signals in the music area so that the children can refer to them.

- Give out instruments and let the children play along with some music. Explain that when it stops they must keep their 'hands quiet'. Allow the children to practise following your directions.

- Watch a video-recording of a conductor and an orchestra, band or choir. Talk about what the conductor might be doing. Stop the tape at relevant points to do this.

- Encourage the children to imitate the actions of the conductor. Describe the conductor as a 'leader' and the orchestra as 'followers'.

40

Role-play

- Assemble a box of instruments and props for a band or orchestra. Include music, music stands, a tape of the relevant music, and clothes such as a coat with tails for the conductor and bow ties. Put a picture of a band or orchestra on the front of the box.

- Decide who will be the conductor or band leader, let them put costumes on and check they are holding their instruments correctly. Position their music. Encourage the 'conductor' and 'musicians' to use and respond to the hand signals as part of the role-play.

Follow the Leader

- Play simple imitation games in which one person leads and the rest follow.

  For example, children take turns to sing or say 'Can you do what I do?' and then demonstrate an action. The others repeat the action while singing or saying:

  'We can do what you do, you do, you do,
  We can do what you do, all day long.'

Sequencing

- Listen to an orchestral piece that starts with one instrument and gradually brings in the whole orchestra, such as Ravel's *Bolero*. Talk about this technique.

- Encourage the children to play in the style they have just heard. Line the players up and ask the conductor to point to each player in turn. Each musician continues playing until all are playing together. The conductor must signal for all to stop at the same time when the music has reached a climax.

- Repeat the above technique, but this time begin with all the players and then stop each player, one by one.

- Group the instruments into types, such as bells, wood blocks and drums. Put each set on a different coloured square of card next to the group of children who will play them. The conductor raises a coloured card and the group with the instruments on the matching coloured card play. They must stop when it is lowered.

- Experiment by encouraging the conductor to use both hands to pick up different combinations of coloured cards.

Home Links

Ask parents or carers to:

- take their children to see music being played live, by street musicians or school orchestras, for example

- join a playgroup and encourage the children to have a music session and play instruments together.

Sounds and Symbols

Starting Points

- Choose a familiar song that would work well with sound effects, such as 'Humpty Dumpty' (crashing sound) and 'Jack and Jill' (footsteps, crashing and tumbling sounds). Discuss the sound effects with the children and experiment with a wide range of instruments.

- Invite musicians into school to play particular types of music. Work in small groups to choose instruments that sound good with the music being played. For example, a classical guitar could accompany a quiet, flowing piece of music, a brass instrument could accompany a march.

Repeat Sequences

- See how many different sounds the children can make using their bodies. Play at putting two sounds together and repeating this sequence as a group, keeping a steady rhythm. For example: clap stamp clap stamp.

- Use other sounds to make a different sequence. For example: pat clap pat clap pat clap.

- Sit in a circle and take turns to make up a different sequence for everyone to repeat. Repeat for sequences of three sounds. For example: clap pat stamp, clap pat stamp.

- Make up symbols for the most popular body sounds and use them to record some of the sequences.

- Make up a sequence by arranging the symbols in a group of two, three or four. Ask the children to follow it with the correct actions.

Rhyme Sequence

- Make up sound effects for a familiar rhyme. Create a display with a collage of the rhyme and the instruments or objects used to make the sounds. For example:

Walking through the jungle and what do I see? I see an elephant walking past me. *(loud footsteps – bongos)*

Walking through the jungle and what do I see? I see a snake sliding past me. *(slithering sounds – sandpaper blocks)*

Walking through the jungle and what do I see? I see a crocodile snapping at me. *(short, loud sounds – wood block)*

Walking through the jungle and what do I see? I see a cricket and he's talking to me. *(clicking sounds – castanets)*

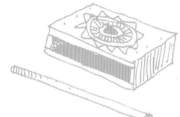

Home Links

Ask parents or carers to:

- read a favourite story aloud, stopping and encouraging their children to make relevant sound effects with various objects

- retell the story to a friend or relative, with their child making the sound effects.

Composing and Representing Sequences

our secret codes
scraper
wood block
shaker

Learning Intentions

- To know that sounds can be represented by marks.

- To understand 'pattern' and 'sequence'.

- To understand that colours and symbols can correspond to individual marks.

- To know that one mark corresponds to one note and that notes and tunes can be represented by a series of marks.

- To know that music is read from left to right.

- To devise and perform simple sequences of sound. To create, read and follow simple sequences.

Starting Points

- Place strips of card and a variety of collage materials (matchsticks, straws, pipe-cleaners, bottle tops, wood shavings) in boxes in a work area.

- Sort the reclaimed materials according to criteria chosen by the children.

- Encourage the children to experiment with instruments and to choose a sound to represent each type of reclaimed material.

- Provide an example of a card containing a sequence of reclaimed materials representing music, with the code and instruments alongside (see photograph above). Challenge the children to try to follow the code and play the music.

Secret Codes

- Help the children to devise their own coded music. For example, a matchstick might represent one beat on the drum, a piece of curly woodshaving might represent maracas shaking. Make a key for your code and put it with your music.

- Use no more than three instruments for each piece of music so the children can quickly memorise the 'secret' codes and play each other's music.

- Develop the children's ability to respond to numbers and to match one action to each mark on the pattern key they have made.

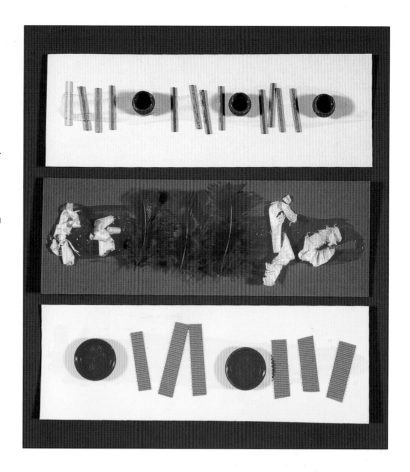

Sound Sequences

- Show the children how to respond to picture cues with a vocal sound effect.

- Make three piles of pictures that the children will recognise and be able to respond to by making a sound, such as three animals or three vehicles.

- Thread string through several pictures to make four small books. Hang the books in a row over a card stand. Encourage the children to turn the pages to make different combinations of a four-part sequence.

- Make tiny picture cards for the children to stick on large square beads. Encourage the children to thread the beads onto string and then sing the pattern they have made.

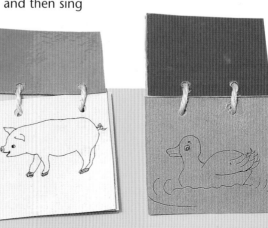

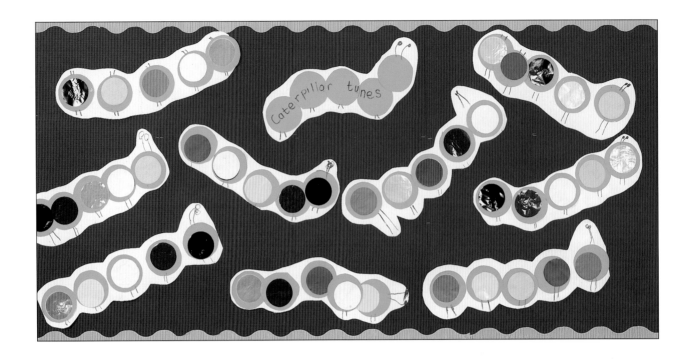

Chime Bar Tunes

- Colour-code each chime bar, if necessary, by adding coloured paper spots. If you have more than one octave and have the same note in high and low pitch, use the same colour for these.

- Glue corresponding colour spots on strips of card to create tunes to be played on the chime bars. Alternatively, use clothes fastening tape, so that the spots can be attached and removed repeatedly.

- Help the children to play a sequence, following the sequence from left to right.

- Make a selection of sequences of songs the children know well. Glue a picture that represents the song on the back of the card. The children can guess and then check the name of the song.

- When children can play sequences of several notes, refer to these as 'tunes'. Let the children swap and play each other's tunes. They may like to give their tune a name. Make a book of the tunes for the children to play.

- Help the children to make a caterpillar or train by sticking large circles or squares in a line. Decorate with details such as legs, eyes or wheels. Add a medium-sized spot or square to each section of the caterpillar or train. When each section has a colour, try playing the sequence on chime bars.

- Put two children's sequences together and see if they can play them.

Representations

- Build up a sequence of sounds related to a series of true events or a story, for example a visit to the seaside. Create a storyboard by illustrating each event. Display the sound-making equipment in front of the pictures.

- Encourage the children to take turns at telling the story and performing the music.

- Sit in an outdoor or garden area. Listen to the sounds that can be heard. Return to the classroom and draw pictures of the sources of the sounds. Find ways of recreating the sounds and make a musical 'collage' of the garden sounds.

- Create a display of pictures of garden sounds and the equipment used to recreate the sounds.

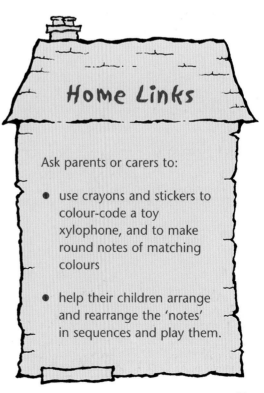

Home Links

Ask parents or carers to:

- use crayons and stickers to colour-code a toy xylophone, and to make round notes of matching colours

- help their children arrange and rearrange the 'notes' in sequences and play them.

Recording Studio

Learning Intentions

- To know that music can be recorded and played back.

- To operate a simple tape recorder.

Starting Points

- Visit a local recording studio and watch a recording being made. If possible, record the children. You could also look at videos of an artist at work in recording studios.

- Develop a recording studio in your role-play area. Provide a battery-powered tape recorder that the children can operate. You will need a few 5- or 10-minute tapes, instruments, microphones and an engineer's baseball cap (for the child whose turn it is to play the role of engineer and operate the tape recorder).

- Discuss the different types of recording (CDs, vinyl, etc.) and look at examples together.

- Create a display of the history of recording, incorporating equipment, recordings and artists from the past.

Role-play

- Discuss what the children saw during their studio visit or on a video. Decide on who will be the performers and who will be the engineer. Let the children choose their instruments and decide if they are making up a tune or a song.

- Practise the piece to be recorded, then let the 'engineer' record it.

- Play back the recording and listen carefully. Does it need to be changed?

- When the children are happy with the recording, store the tape in the music area and let other children listen to it.

- Encourage the children to decorate the cassette boxes for easy identification.

- Make a book about this work, showing the sequence of events, including the choice of instruments, practising the music and recording and re-recording. This could include photographs or drawings by the children.

Home Links

Ask parents or carers to:

- gather pictures of recording artists from magazines to bring into school for display.

Appreciating and Responding to Music

Learning Intentions

- To appreciate and respond to music by dancing, moving and performing.

- To show how they feel about music through facial expression, mime or dance.

- To interpret music and convey their understanding through art work.

- To develop skills in associating music with emotions, actions and visual images.

Starting Points

- Build up your own library of 5- to 10-minute tapes with short descriptions and project-related ideas on the front of the cases. Sources can include compilation CD recordings, recommendations by classical music radio stations or music books for young children. Include different styles of classical music and popular music.

- A music library could include the following classical music:

Happy/lively
'Anitra's dance' from *Peer Gynt* by Grieg
'Peter's tune' from *Peter and the Wolf* by Prokofiev
'Fossils' from *Carnival of Animals* by Saint-Saëns
'Joy to the World' by Handel

Calming/relaxing
'Dream children' by Elgar
'Morning' from *Peer Gynt* by Grieg
The 'Swan' from *Carnival of Animals* by Saint Saëns
'Greensleeves' by Vaughan Williams

Frightening/mysterious
'In the hall of the Mountain King' from *Peer Gynt* by Grieg
Danse Macabre from *Carnival of Animals* by Saint-Saëns

- Include memorable music with repetitive passages in the music library. This will be more accessible and easier to listen to. As such, it will make an excellent resource when introducing the music library to the children. (See page 64 for suggestions of other types of music.)

We all chose our favourite type of music

Happy music

Calm music

Frightening music

Listening Times

- Begin by establishing a regular listening time, for example at the end of each session or in the children's snack/milk area.

- Introduce a piece of music for each week, so that the children begin to recognise particular pieces. At the end of the week, put a copy of the music in the music area with a suitable player.

- Encourage the children to listen to short pieces of music just for enjoyment. At this stage, do not feel that you have to ask them to describe or respond to the music. However, do reinforce any attempts they may make with praise and recognition.

- Encourage the children to help you label the music they have listened to with a description of how the music made them feel. Illustrate boxes for CDs or cassettes with appropriate pictures.

- Listen to compilations of music that evoke particular feelings. How does the music make the children feel? Listen to 'happy', 'calm' and 'frightening' music. Which kind of music do the children like best? Make a graph with the children to discover which type of music is the most popular (see photograph above).

- Encourage the children to react physically to the music, focusing on facial expressions, mime and dance.

- When children have had a lot of experience listening to music, use a piece of music as a stimulus to develop work across the curriculum, as described in the following pages.

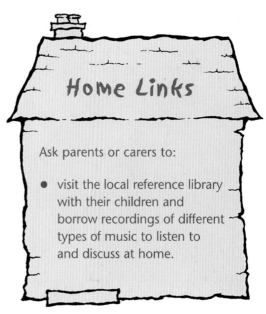

Home Links

Ask parents or carers to:

- visit the local reference library with their children and borrow recordings of different types of music to listen to and discuss at home.

Project One - Bees

Learning Intentions

- To listen to and enjoy a piece of music.

- To extend expressive vocabulary.

- To observe living things.

- To represent life and movement in art.

- To use a computer to create patterns and shapes.

- To move sensitively to music.

Starting Points

- Listen to the stimulus music: the 'Flight of the Bumble Bee' by Rimsky-Korsakov.

- Talk about the music and ask the children to describe some of its basic elements: 'Was it fast/slow, loud/soft, high/low?' Write the words they use on individual pieces of card for a display.

- Put a recording of the music in the music area for the children to listen to. In a neighbouring book corner, display books containing stories about or pictures of bees.

Activities

- Listen to the stimulus music again before taking the children outside into a garden area. Take a tape recorder with you and play the music outside. Ask the children to find any sounds outside that are similar to the sounds in the music.

- Listen to the music again. Display a collection of percussion instruments. Find instruments that make a buzzing sound and use them to play along with the music.

- Make kazoos by folding tracing paper over clean combs. Encourage the children to play them to make buzzing sounds.

- Arrange a visit to a local beekeeper or watch a video or slides of bees making honey and honey being collected.

- Listen to the music after watching some bees. Ask questions to help the children describe how the bees move: 'Do they move in straight lines? In curves? In squiggles? In circles?'

- Talk about and try to make sounds to represent the low constant buzz of a flying bee and the high-pitched vibrating sound of a bee collecting pollen.

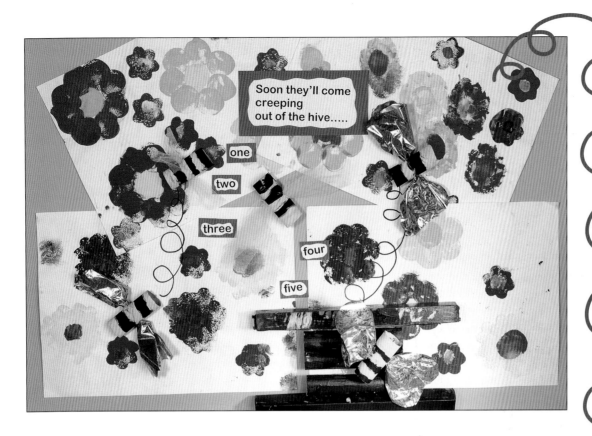

Soon they'll come creeping out of the hive.....

one
two
three
four
five

- Use cardboard tubes, black and yellow paints, pipe-cleaners and Cellophane pieces to make bees.

- Let the children make their bee move in the air while the music is playing.

- Help each child to make their 'flight path' shape on the paper, using a thick felt-tipped pen. Fix each child's bee on its own 'flight path'.

- Use a paint program on the computer. Let each child control a mouse, roller ball or touch screen to create pictures of the bee's flight path. Print it out in colour to add to the bee display.

- Make a 3D beehive from recycled materials and add it to your display.

- Show the children some different types of honey to smell and taste. Use the honey to make honey sandwiches. Compare the tasks of using runny and set honey.

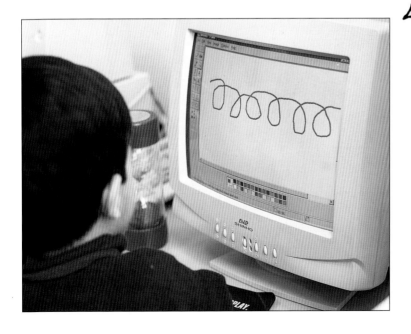

Home Links

Ask parents or carers to:

- take their children to a garden or park to watch bees gather pollen

- encourage their children to copy the sounds the bees make

- borrow a recording of the stimulus music from a library and listen to it with their children.

Project Two - Storms

Learning Intentions

- To learn about weather types.

- To extend vocabulary about the weather.

- To listen to and appreciate music.

- To represent the weather in art.

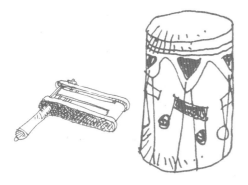

we listened to thunderstorm by Richard Strauss

the storm

whoosh

splash

Starting Points

- Listen to the stimulus music: 'Thunderstorm', from *An Alpine Symphony*, op. 64 by Richard Strauss.

- If possible, begin the project on a stormy day. Watch and listen to the sounds and sights of the storm.

It's raining again

Monday Tuesday Wednesday Thursday Friday

- Record the weather on a chart. Collect and measure the rainfall during your session time and compare it with the following days.

- In your listening time, introduce the music explaining that it was written to make people think of a storm. The entire piece is over three minutes, so you may decide to listen to part of the music.

Activities

- Put a recording of the music in the music area. Encourage the children to listen to it over a week.

- After listening to the entire piece of music, ask the children what they could hear and what the music made them think about. Display their key words with visual symbols (see photograph below).

- Paste the key words and paintings onto a large piece of paper the colour of a stormy sky to create a 'storm' display.

- Listen to the music again, and then just to short bursts of the music. Can the children hear the thunder, lightning and driving rain? Is the rain heavy all the time? Is there thunder all the time? How does the thunder make them feel?

- Encourage the children to make their own storm sounds using a selection of instruments. Add the best 'storm-sound' instruments to your 'storm' display.

- Decide on colours, patterns and shapes that represent heavy rain, storm clouds, lightning, puddles, splashes and so on. For rain, try using thick paint and thin brushes on pieces of Cellophane. Dry these flat overnight, then place them on top of the 'storm' display paper.

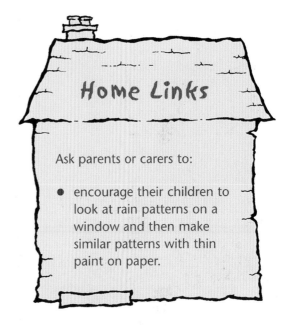

Home Links

Ask parents or carers to:

- encourage their children to look at rain patterns on a window and then make similar patterns with thin paint on paper.

- Encourage the children to make their own storm music using instruments from the display, singing or other vocal effects. Record the music and add the tape to the display, along with the Strauss recording.

we made a storm picture

ash bang

make some storm music

We listened to music and heard lots of things

cellos · birds · violins · scrapers · drums · waves · storms · seas · triangles · wind · trumpets

Project Three - Fountains

Learning Intentions

- To explore and record features of the local environment.

- To operate a camera.

- To listen to music, to compose music and to represent music in art work.

- To extend the children's expressive and descriptive language.

- To become familiar with the properties of different materials.

Starting Points

- Take the children on a walk to a park, garden or town square where there is a working fountain. Watch the fountain and listen to the sounds. Encourage the children to take photographs of the fountain (provide a simple camera that is easy to operate).

- During the walk, note down the places you pass and the location of the fountain. Later, the children can illustrate the directions and major landmarks on their journey.

- Listen to some of the stimulus music *Jeux d'eau* by Ravel in your listening time. Explain that it is called 'The Fountains'. Ask the children to describe what they can hear. Write down some of the key words and phrases and use them throughout the following activities.

- Use wateplay equipment and junk materials to build a fountain in your water tray. Add blue food-colouring to the water. Listen to the sound of the water drops. Make a list of words to describe the sounds that can be made by water as it pours or drops.

our map of our walk

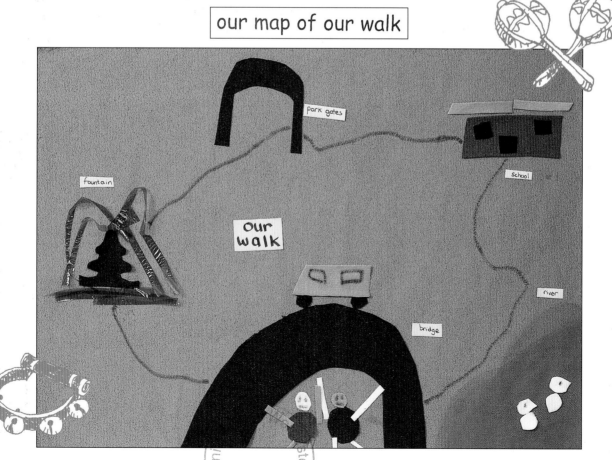

- Paint watercolour pictures of flowing water while the music is playing. Add glitter to represent sparkling water.

- Wash pieces of paper with a thin paint-and-water solution. Provide plastic droppers to drop very small quantities of stronger and more concentrated colours onto the wet sheets or onto blotting paper. Compare and contrast the effects.

- Display the pictures in a 'fountain' display, along with photographs of the fountain you visited.

- Choose some instruments to represent the sounds made by a fountain. Place these by the display with invitations for the children to make 'fountain' music. Add some of the words used by the children during the week.

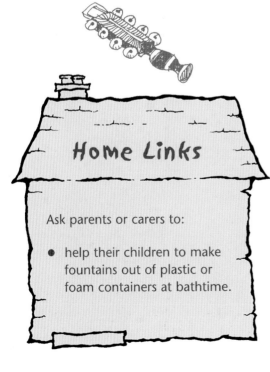

Home Links

Ask parents or carers to:

- help their children to make fountains out of plastic or foam containers at bathtime.

Project Four - Patterns and Shapes

Learning Intentions

- To move according to the speed and volume of a piece of music.

- To compare the timbre of two different pieces of music.

- To extend descriptive vocabulary and use of imagery.

- To develop painting techniques, including the use of colour and space.

- To develop the use of pattern and colour in painting.

- To explore direction, width and length.

'Jupiter'

- Listen to some of the stimulus music, such as Holst's 'Jupiter' from *The Planets suite*, during listening time. Ask the children to describe the music. Introduce words such as 'fairly loud', 'majestic', 'strong' and 'flowing'.

- Encourage the children to move their arms to the music. Do they move their hands up and down sharply or in a flowing pattern? Discuss the speed and volume of the music and write down key words.

Pavane

- Provide some strong colours and a variety of implements for making broad, strong strokes. Play the stimulus music and remind the children of the way their arms moved to the music. Encourage them to paint the colour and shape of the music.

- Cut crêpe paper into long thin pieces to make streamers. Tape one end of the streamers to a stick. As the music is playing, encourage the children to make arm patterns while holding the streamers. Develop the arm movements into a dance involving whole body movements.

- Photograph the patterns made by the streamers and add these to the music in the art area as a stimulus for the children to create more impressions of the music.

- Listen to the stimulus music, Ravel's *Pavane pour une infante défunte* (Dance for a dead princess), during listening time. Ask the children to describe it. This is a fairly slow piece with a light dancing feel to each note.

- Encourage the children to compare it with Holst's 'Jupiter'. What sort of movements will the children make with their hands and arms to *Pavane*? How are these movements different to those they made during 'Jupiter'?

- Look at some of the children's paintings of the 'Jupiter' music. How will paintings of *Pavane* differ? Choose suitable colours to express the word 'light'. Let the children experiment by adding white to colours to make them lighter. Experiment with a variety of dabbing techniques using sponges on sticks, cotton buds and finger tips, while *Pavane* is playing.

- Experiment with whole body movements to express the feelings and rhythm of the music.

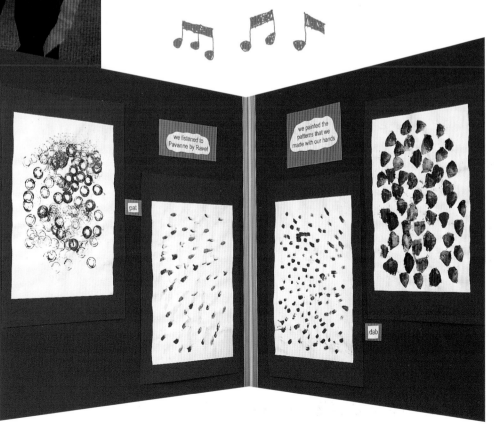

we listened to Pavanne by Ravel

we painted the patterns that we made with our hands

pat

dab

Gymnopédie No. 3

● Listen to the stimulus music, Erik Satie's *Gymnopédie No. 3*. This piece is slow, with a flowing repetitive melody. Agree on words to describe the piece.

● Ask the children to use their hands or their whole arms to draw the pattern of the music in the air.

● Think of things that can move quietly, smoothly and slowly (for example, fish, birds, balloons, clouds).

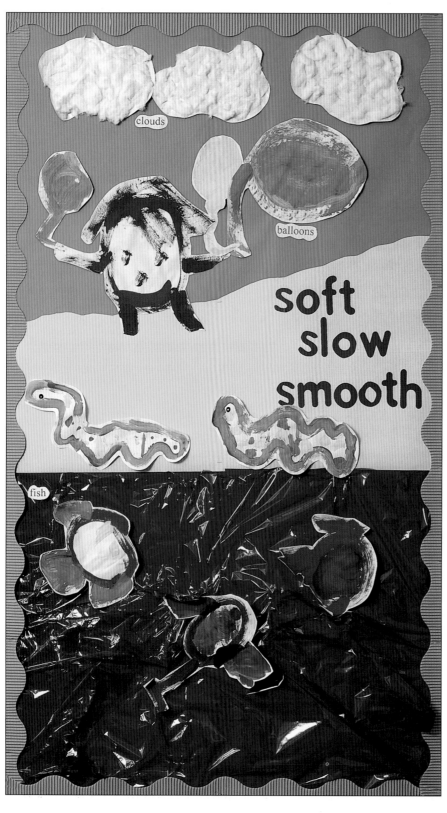

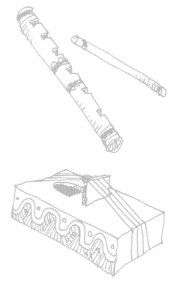

● Encourage the children to paint pictures to illustrate the movement and feel of the piece.

● During a movement session, encourage the children to move to a fast bouncy piece of music, such as 'Fossils' from *Carnival of Animals* by Saint-Saëns, then to Satie's piece. Experiment with whole body movements to express both pieces.

● In the music area, investigate ways of playing the same instrument in a fast, loud, bouncy style and then in a slow, soft, smooth style.

● Make bubbles in a container by blowing through a straw into water mixed with washing-up liquid. Watch the bubbles float while the music plays.

'Memories'

- Listen to Francisco Tarrega's 'Memories of the Alhambra'. This is a quiet, reflective classical guitar piece. The constant soft and very fast plucking of the strings creates a shimmering effect. Talk about the music and agree on key words to describe it.

- Spread paper over a large area of the floor and suspend an upturned salt pot filled with coloured sand or salt above it. Ask the children to watch quietly and listen to the music. Push the suspended pot so that it swings slowly, making a pattern on the paper.

- Let the children mix new, soft shades to illustrate the music. They can mix these by adding a small amount of powder paint to the sand or salt. Set the salt pot moving again to make the pattern multi-coloured. Photograph the result for display.

- Provide a variety of granular and powdered materials. Encourage the children to experiment to see which materials pour easily from small containers or funnels and which do not.

- Add powder paint to the granular materials and create a textured painting by dropping the coloured mixtures onto a thin film of glue over paper. Play the stimulus music as they create the soft, shimmering pictures.

- Invite a classical guitarist to come to play for the children. Let the children experiment with the strings and investigate how they work. Provide hollow containers and elastic bands for children to experiment with pitch and volume.

We listened to "Air on a G String" by Bach.

zig zags an[d] down

up and down round and round

up down and across

we p[aint] patte[rn]

listening, pain[t] and collage

'Air on a G String'

- Listen to the stimulus music, JS Bach's 'Air on a G String' during listening time. This piece is strong, slow and smooth, with a definite walking beat. Ask children to walk their hands on the floor while listening. Discuss how they might be feeling if they were walking like this.

- Use the rhythm of the beat to help the children 'draw' squares in the air. Say: 'Up-across-down' as the children trace the shape with whole arm movements. Then encourage the children to do the same movements but with just a wrist and hand.

and

the
made
ur arms

up and down

We listened to "Air on a G String" by Bach.

a dinosaur walks slow like this Seema

a snail is slow and soft Amir

listening , painting and collage

- As the music plays, experiment with painting strokes – up and down, across and back. Encourage the children to find colours that represent the mood of the music.

- Using stick-shaped collage pieces, such as straws, pipe-cleaners and lolly sticks, make collage pictures in the style of the paintings.

- Draw, paint, trace and print more square shapes using a wide variety of equipment. Provide visual models for the children to draw from close observation. Display with paintings and collage work.

- Look at video footage of different animals moving. Ask: 'Which animals walk in a similar way to the beat in the music?' Paint pictures of the animals for display.

- Play the stimulus music and encourage the children to walk with their hands, and then with their feet. Ask: 'Are your steps slow or fast, heavy or light?' 'Can you move like the animals that you have been watching?'

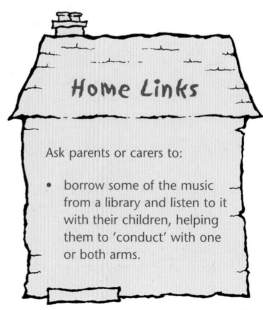

Home Links

Ask parents or carers to:

- borrow some of the music from a library and listen to it with their children, helping them to 'conduct' with one or both arms.

Music for the Listening Area

An effective way of gathering a wide variety of music is to collect compilation CDs of classical, jazz and popular music. Listed below are just a few suggestions for putting together a varied music library – a start point from which you can explore whole worlds of music. Many of these compilations, or similar compilations, are produced by specialist companies such as 'Space Craft', and are available on the internet.

Calm Music

- *Cascade* – Terry Oldfield
- *Crystal Healing* – Anthony Miles
- *Edge of Dreams* – Phil Thornton
- *Evening Stillness* – Anthony Miles
- *The Fairy Ring* – Mike Rouland
- *Harmony* – David Sun
- *The Healing Harp* – Patricia Spero
- *Music for Children* – Anthony Miles

Energetic Music

- *Lifeforce* – Stuart Jones

Mysterious/Inspiring Music

- *Alien Encounter* – Phil Thornton
- *Eagle Spirit* – Medwyn Goodall
- *Reverence* – Terry Oldfield

Ethnic Music

- *Great Spirit* (Native American) – Mel Goodall
- *Native American Dream* (compilation)
- *Rharoe* – Phil Thornton
- *Spirit of Africa* – Terry Oldfield
- *Spirit of the Rainforest* – Terry Oldfield

Music and the Natural World

- *Out of the Depths* (whale song) – Terry Oldfield
- *The Way of the Ocean* – Medwyn Goodall

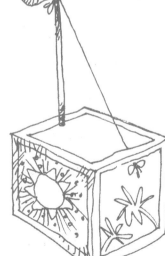